SEASON
OF
REAPING

Fourth Book in the Seasons of Our Lives Collection

REVEREND LARRY L. CAMPER

WestBow Press books may be ordered through booksellers or by contacting:

WestBow Press
A Division of Thomas Nelson & Zondervan
1663 Liberty Drive
Bloomington, IN 47403
www.westbowpress.com
844-714-3454

Interior Image Credit: Timothy Brown

Unless otherwise indicated, All Scripture quotations are taken from the King James Version, public domain.

Scripture quotation marked (NKJV) taken from the New King James Version. Copyright © 1982 by Thomas Nelson, Inc. Used by permission. All rights reserved.

ISBN: 979-8-3850-4125-1 (sc)
ISBN: 979-8-3850-4124-4 (e)

Library of Congress Control Number: 2024927250

Print information available on the last page.

WestBow Press rev. date: 01/14/2025

WESTBOW
PRESS®
A DIVISION OF THOMAS NELSON
& ZONDERVAN

Table of Contents

Biography - Reverend Larry L. Camper

Reverend Larry L. Camper was born on June 7, 1957 in the small town of Seaford, Delaware. Being raised in a very rural town, he developed a sincere appreciation of time spent with family and friends. He still places great value on family and friends today. As a child and teen he was a member of Seaford's East Clarence Street Church of God where his mother, grandparents, and great-grandparents were or had been members, and where his personal relationship with Jesus had its humble but deeply rooted beginning. He attended Seaford schools until graduating from Seaford Senior High School in 1975. As a senior in high school Reverend Camper was selected to *Who's Who* among American High School students and upon graduating traveled to Europe, spending the summer in Sweden as an American Field Service exchange student. As a rurally raised young man, upon his return to the U. S. he became a college student in Ohio, some six hundred miles from home and nearly forgot the God-loving, God-revering way in which he had been raised. Even though God had His great hand on Reverend Camper's life, for a long time, he wanted to do his own thing. He wanted to do things his way, the way his flesh was leading him, instead of God's way.

But God! God has changed that. He blessed Reverend Camper to surrender his life to Christ. He has also blessed him with a wonderful family; a God-fearing, God-loving, beautiful, and compassionate wife, three terrific grown children, and four absolutely terrific grandchildren. Since the publishing of his first three books, "…*if* You Faint Not", "Season of Hope", and "Season of Sowing in Excellence", Reverend Camper has seen his oldest daughter, Lauren, experience numerous promotions and become a Training Educator in a large international Health Maintenance Organization (HMO). She is also the proud owner of her first home, a brand-new home. His middle child, Deidre, now equipped with her Master's Degree in Human Service Administration, is enjoying a fresh new virtual teaching experience, working with elementary-aged children. Larry Jr., the youngest, and only son is enjoying his work as an art handler and is still spending a good amount of his time doing what he loves as an artist, painting.

Reverend Camper was blessed to be a member of New Mount Olive Baptist Church from April of 1990 to October of 2011. There he served as a deacon, taught Sunday Adult Bible Institute, and shared in the teaching of Bible Study (called "Word Alive"). He is thankful for and loved his church family and is especially grateful to God for the teaching and preaching of his former pastor, Reverend Dr. Luke Mitchell Jr. Reverend Camper was one of the assistants to the pastor and for ten years was usually in the studios of 1340 AM-WYCB Radio on Friday evenings from 7:30 to 8:00 for the New Mount Olive broadcast of *"Higher Ground."* He shared his poetry during the church's broadcast for thirteen years, starting about three years before he started coming into the studio. Reverend Camper has had poetry available in several local bookstores. He and his wife, Debra, together, were the coordinators of the Marriage Enrichment Ministry at New Mount Olive. The two of them along with all three of their children joined Kettering Baptist Church where Reverend Camper has served as an associate minister, the coordinator of the Senior's Ministry, and the Minister of Visitation. His wife, Debra has been a part of the dance ministry, works with the website team, and by profession is an IT Specialist. Reverend Camper sits under the teaching, preaching, and leadership of a truly gifted and anointed pastor, Bucas Sterling III. He has completed his studies at Lancaster Bible College in Greenbelt, Maryland, and received his Bachelor's in Biblical Studies in December of 2014.

Reverend Camper has been very active in his community and over the years especially enjoyed helping out at his children's schools. He loves his quiet morning devotions and was licensed and preached his initial sermon on June 4, 2004 and was ordained on June 2, 2007. Reverend Camper loves writing and God blessed him to start *In Due Season Ministries*…a ministry through which Reverend Camper desires to communicate the Gospel through sermons and other means. He loves writing plays that inspire and encourage and was blessed that at New Mount Olive and Kettering he was given opportunities to write, direct, and act in numerous plays that were presented at each church. He would sometimes take part as an actor in the plays that God gave him and even took advantage of the opportunity to be onstage with a fairly good-sized part in a play at his local theater playing both a bailiff and juror. This book is the fourth of five in his series, "Seasons of Our Lives". He also looks forward to writing curriculum for Christian Publishers. Reverend Camper is praying for continued personal growth in ministry to help him with both preaching and writing all those things which God places in his heart to be a blessing to His people. He loves his writing ministry, but thanks God that he is a preacher first and considers himself blessed to be a writer in addition to the privilege of preaching the gospel—as a communicator of the Gospel. He counts himself privileged by every preaching and writing opportunity he is blessed with.

DEDICATION

I thank God for the people He has placed in my life, having been blessed in multiple ways by their presence. One person who has seriously and positively impacted my walk with the Lord is my pastor, Pastor Bucas Sterling III. Having sat under his teaching for thirteen years, I have learned so much about being a follower of Christ. I am a much better servant, minister, husband, father, and man because of his teaching, preaching, and leadership. I see Pastor Sterling as a Pastor who loves the Lord and loves the sheep that God has placed under his care. When I first came to Kettering, I would often tell Pastor how much I appreciated his preaching, teaching, and leadership. His response was always the same, always —*"To God be the Glory"*. Whenever I would go on any ministry engagement, I felt well-prepared because of the teaching I had received and example I had in Pastor Bucas Sterling III, truly a gifted preacher, teacher, and leader. I sincerely thank God for my pastor and for his wife alongside him, our awesome first lady, Carolyn Sterling.

INTRODUCTION

Have you ever noticed how sometimes in life things just seem to sneak up on you? Yes, it seems to me that there are times when, without realizing it, you look around and see that things have changed, sometimes by the grace of God, for the better. This is exactly what has happened in this great season of my life. After landing at a place where there was an abundance of incredible preaching, teaching, and leading opportunities, I truly began to grow both in my walk with the Lord and, so very importantly also, in my understanding of the Word of God. I started to understand much more about this precious gift called life and about one's spiritual life. With much joy, I started to find myself taking on challenges that I would normally have avoided. I seriously began to do a much better job at most every task I accepted. Now, please understand that I didn't just take on any and every thing. It seems somehow that I even started accepting (wait for it) the right tasks, not necessarily the ones that were easy or convenient. Soon, I began to actually find myself getting (more) things done. This was certainly new territory for me. After doing things pretty well for a stretch (at least much better than before), and without me recognizing it, I was accomplishing a number of things on a fairly consistent basis. God was working through me and I was being blessed as I was being used increasingly by God to accomplish ministry in the area He had gifted me to operate. Just because He is God, (absolutely no goodness of my own) I was soon experiencing blessing after blessing, the greatest being just the pure joy of doing what God had gifted/ equipped me to do. Doing what I needed to do to take care of my family financially the way I should had not by any means been my strong suit. But then as time went on, I started to see Debra being able to get and do some of the things she needed or needed to do and even some of the things that she desired or desired to do. The Camper family was being blessed in numerous ways. I am so very grateful to God that now I do believe that I (even undeserving Larry, that I) am being used by God to make a difference in the kingdom. That is the true joy of reaping—to just begin to understand that God has prepared you for a great work and then find yourself being used by Him to begin to do things you really didn't see yourself ever being able to do. Doing these things, while recognizing that it is only in God's great strength that any good thing is accomplished is a big part of what makes their accomplishment so great. After my stormy season, season of hope, and season of sowing in excellence, this reaping season I find myself in truly amazes me. To see God use me the way He is and to bless me the way He has, to me is nothing short of well, AMAZING! I guess that makes sense…His amazing grace! All the blessings I didn't earn, don't deserve, and could not see for myself. Welcome to my Season of Reaping!

Acknowledgments

Very near and dear to my heart is a couple that Debra and I have been blessed to know for about 35 years, **Charlie and Minnie Bell**. They are two of the kindest people you could ever meet. We served as co-laborers and worshipped with the Bells and were blessed to see them and witness up close their great love for God, for each other, for the people of God, and for family. Even though we now live several states apart, we have stayed in touch with each other and from time to time will actually get together. When we visit them in North Carolina we are greeted with that great southern hospitality that we have become accustomed to from them. Deb and I respect them for being a loving, classy couple and our very dear friends.

I truly thank God for one of the most giving people one could ever meet. Debra and I are so very blessed that we were able to meet and get to know Ms. **Mary B. King**, "Ma King" as we lovingly call her. I believe she enjoys us calling her that, but many more than just Deb and me call her *Ma King*. In fact, it just might be a tossup between the number of people that called her "Sister King" and those that call her "Ma King". There is a very good and real reason for that. She always causes those around her to know the love of a mother...that is because if you're blessed to spend any time around her, she would care for you not just in word, but also in deed, as one would for their own child. I remember when Deb and I moved into the home we now live in, she put poor ole Deacon King to work as she and he surprised us and came over with some serious groceries...I mean a lot of trips back and forth to the truck getting more and more groceries. That was a number of years ago, but to this day, even though she is no longer in the D.C. area we stay in touch, generally speaking by phone at least a few times a month.

John Cancelleri is someone who I have considered a dear friend since I first met him in 1975, the year we both graduated from High School. We met at Findlay College, in Findlay, Ohio where we became freshmen that year. John was from New Jersey and I would travel back and forth from Ohio to my home in Delaware and sometimes to visit with his family in North Bergen, New Jersey. Our complexions were different but our hearts weren't. John and I still laugh about how he added diversity to the bridal party when Debra and I renewed our wedding vows for our "Sweet 16" celebration at New Mount Olive Baptist Church. Even though we met nearly 50 years ago, we are still in touch with each other, speaking just about monthly. John and his lovely bride Heidi, love the Lord and have done a lot of work in the missions field and have raised numerous children who were not theirs biologically. I truly thank God for blessing me with the opportunity to know John as a very dear friend and brother in Christ.

When Debra and I joined our current church, we were pretty sad because we loved New Mount Olive Baptist Church and the church family we were leaving behind and some of the close relationships that come with being "Church Family". We knew that in time we would again know the joy of being close to the people we worship with. There are a number of members at Kettering Baptist Church that Deb and I are very close to. Miss **Marion Dickson** is one of those people. I have never known a more giving person. So much of her energy goes into doing what she does for other people. I've been blessed at Kettering to do a number of things in ministry. Sister Dickson has been such a tremendous help in most of those endeavors. She is always thinking of our family and being a blessing to us. If she sees something she thinks our now 5-year-old granddaughter, Khloé would enjoy she gets it and calls to say "I'm gonna drop something off at your house, but you don't have to come out or anything. I'll just ring the doorbell and leave it". That's the way she rolls...never looking for a response, just loving people. I love writing and doing plays and one of the folks that I have enjoyed being a part of those plays as a brilliant actress is Sister Marion Dickson. Debra and I really are grateful to have Sister Dickson in our lives.

Timothy Brown and I met about twenty years ago at New Mount Olive Baptist Church. In Tim, I see a man of God whom I have the utmost of respect for and who's life has been a great example for me. When I consider the person that he is, I am blessed. Tim is one of the most considerate, encouraging, and kind people I have ever met. Here is the part that is really important for me—He is also one of the strongest examples of a Christian, man, husband, father as one would ever find. As I see him leading his family, I am blessed! He and his loving and gifted wife, Corrin, along with their three children are a true blessing to their community to their church, and literally to the world, as they are fulltime missionaries and all three of their young children have travelled the world doing missionary work. Tim probably doesn't even understand how much of a major impact he has had on my life. I remember how about 15 or so years ago at our old church, not only were he and I working together playing basketball with the young guys, but he was also instrumental in helping with the producing and directing of the plays God blessed me to write at New Mount Olive Baptist Church. That part, him being a great blessing in terms of theater, continued at Kettering Baptist Church. I truly thank God for my brother, my friend, Tim Brown and his family.

Season of Reaping Story

God has been good to me. It feels so good to be able to sincerely say that He has blessed me beyond what I would have ever imagined for myself. He truly has. As I started writing this "Season of Our Lives" series, I knew very intimately, a season of struggle. Being in that season of struggle is the very thing that prompted me to start (purposely) writing. After writing (and living what I was writing about) for a good while, I felt grateful to recognize my stormy season of struggle beginning to change. I welcomed and embraced a season of hope as I experienced it beginning to peak through what seemed to be the darkest of clouds. This wasn't hope for God to bless me with any kind of material thing, "stuff", or abundance. It was simply the glimmer of hope that there was a possibility of the coming of days when I wasn't going mad with worry! Yes, you read that right, just *a glimmer of a hope of a possibility*. Indeed, it would have felt good to have or to experience or recognize abundant hope even in the midst of my season of struggle, but I didn't. For a time, I saw virtually nothing that I recognized as a lasting or serious reason to hope. By the grace of God, when it did come, I gratefully welcomed this season of hope. I even saw God's hand in my life (knowing it had to be His hand) as He blessed me to begin to do some things differently, to do them in a better way. I actually started to experience a season of operating in excellence (especially compared to the way I had been doing things). God was growing me and I could see and feel the difference that growth was making. Yes, I am able to see, to recognize that God has truly blessed me. He has indeed, been good to me. Even as God was allowing me to know the seasons in my life, the first three were pretty easy to either recognize (in the case of my season of struggle), and to then in the case of season of hope, and season of sowing in excellence, imagine, enter, and to walk into. But to truly expect to see or to envision or imagine a season of reaping would be something that I would truly need help with. Not having been one to practice excellence, I had never really had reason to envision a season of reaping—especially if it was going to follow a season of sowing in excellence. I did know that *reaping "good"* had something to do with and came on the other end of *sowing "good"*. I had not been used to sowing in excellence or anything that resembles excellence. But *blessing me* is just what God has done. He has been a great blessing in my life. He has truly been good to me and I recognize that I am now experiencing an incredible season of reaping. I really am! I am so grateful to God that I am able to recognize, to see, to distinguish (even upon examination) how He is blessing me (I believe in a special way). Please make sure you do not overlook this season in your life, your season of reaping when—God truly blesses!

About thirteen years ago my wife and I joined Kettering Baptist Church. Having left a church family that we loved dearly, we were very sad when we left those who had become family to us, the people we worshiped with, knew, and loved. We noticed in our first few weeks at Kettering that we were truly being fed the Word of God through the expository preaching of our pastor, Pastor Bucas Sterling III. Still, we were missing our church family from our previous church. That local church and branch of Zion had been our church home for over 21 years. At the same time, we felt the impact of God's speaking to us that came from the Word of God through the pulpit and Pastor Sterling every Sunday at Kettering. What we were hearing being preached Sunday after Sunday was <u>what God said in His Word</u>! As much as we missed our old church family, we were at the same time growing from the Spiritual nourishment we were being blessed with through Pastor Sterling and this expository style of preaching. The very first Sunday we attended Kettering Baptist Church, we knew without a doubt, it was the church home for us. We had been very concerned about being able to find a new church that would become our church home. After hearing Pastor Sterling preach the Word on that first Sunday, we knew our church search was over. We weren't "churchless" any more. While we were not yet familiar with our new church family members, before long that too changed. The strong expository preaching that we were hearing landed on our hearts, hearts that God had prepared, and was beginning to change. I was beginning to see things differently. I was also beginning to walk differently. Interestingly, our church theme at Kettering Baptist Church Legacy Center for 2023 was "Walking in the Power of the Holy Spirit". I am not claiming to have gotten everything together all at once (or even to this point). But I surely have grown in my walk with the Lord, sitting under the preaching, teaching, and leadership of Pastor Bucas Sterling III and our awesome First Lady, Carolyn Sterling.

I am understanding that this season of reaping is very much tied to my season of sowing. God has allowed me to grow tremendously in my walk with Him and in the way He has blessed me to begin to live my life. I believe that because of that growth, the door through which God intends to bless others using me has been opened. I believe that in His blessing others through me, He has decided to bless me as well. This is my season of reaping.

There is no way I deserve, or can take any credit for all or for any good thing that God has done in my life. He has done a lot. Even in my writing this *story* my eyes are being opened to just how much He's done. The place I must start however is in what God has done with my formerly major problem (now not nearly as major of a problem) of not being disciplined or consistent. I truly hope that you are not stuck on this—but maybe you know someone who every year on January 1st starts the trek on attempting to make real whatever resolution he or she had decided on for that particular year.

By way of example, allow me to share with you just some of what God has done in my life. One of the numerous things I appreciate regarding my former pastor, Pastor Luke Mitchell Jr. for, is teaching me the importance of devotion time with Jesus. He emphasized the importance of taking notes (especially of things which impacted or spoke to me) as I study the Word of God. He also shared with me the importance of periodically reviewing those notes. I review some part of my notes every day. By the grace of God, I have been blessed with an abundance of free time (even when free time was not what I wanted or felt that I needed). Because of the amount of free time I had, I was able to devote a good bit of time to the study of the Word. I know that I am not the fastest one to learn—but I am able to learn. One thing, however that (by choice) I had never done a whole lot of, was reading. No, I wasn't the one to just pick up a book (any book) and read even a couple of pages of it. But I started, at the conclusion of my daily devotion time, to read. I started reading things that were helpful for me being able to do the things I needed to and should be able to do. I have not made a New Year's resolution for the last three or four years. What the Lord has blessed me to do since October 1, 2007, however, is to for a very high percentage of those days, have a wonderful full, rich devotion time…in the Word. Then (here is the book-reading key because) at the end of my devotion time He has even blessed me to (wait for it) "read". I share this with you because I see this as a tremendous blessing. God has given me the time to read. But equally if not more importantly, He has not only given me the desire to be in His Word this way, but as a bonus, He has allowed me to read and learn other things as well. To have been as consistent in anything (for me) as I have been in terms of devotion (and now, reading) has been a great blessing. But for this activity to bless me to be gaining more knowledge and understanding and truth that I can use to know my Savior and walk more closely with Him…well that's the ticket! So *yes, this is my season of reaping.* This daily diet of the Word along with the biblical teaching and preaching I am receiving at Kettering Baptist Church is truly changing my life. Hey, wait a minute, isn't that what the Word of God does? Indeed, yes, that is what the Word does. Hebrews 4:12 says, *"For the Word of God is living and powerful, and sharper than any two-edged sword, piercing even to the division of soul and spirit, and of joints and marrow, and is a discerner of the thoughts and intents of the heart (NKJV)."* The Word of God changes you! God is doing so many awesome things in my life, but to be able to be in His Word consistently, and for this long, has been a total blessing. I find myself anxious to get to my study to spend that couple of hours or so with Him in devotion. He opens my eyes, allowing me to learn and to grow in my time with Him, with His Word, but I believe He also uses these times to simply posture my heart and mind to hear Him more clearly at other times as well. I am so grateful to see that the season of reaping Jesus had in store for me deals more with my spiritual life than it does with anything else. However, I am grateful for the "anything else" that I am learning (from reading) regarding things around the house and other general, helpful bits of information to help to live life more ably.

It just may be that your season of reaping is in some way your season of waking up. In my life I am realizing now that I am blessed and how very much I am blessed. Perhaps God has blessed you with what you need to do His will and maybe even some of what you want. Now, armed with those things you, like me, may have awakened to what you do have and more importantly awakened to how much you have grown in your walk with the Lord and in part because of that, how much more He will be able to use you for the kingdom work He has for you! You feel blessed because you see clearly where you need to improve and know that it is simply a matter of listening for (and obeying) Jesus' voice and knowing that He has positioned you by allowing the things you need to come your way—for you to achieve His purpose for your life! I thank God that He has allowed me to be blessed so—to reap this way.

He made this very clear to me as my wife and I took one of our one-night monthly getaways. We had started this practice about seven months before and on our eighth monthly retreat (only about 20 miles from our home) the Lord spoke very clearly to my heart. He made it clear that He had positioned me through a season of sowing in excellence (especially alongside the way I had been doing things) and was moving me into reaping and that I was truly being positioned for the achieving of His purpose for my life. In staying transparent, or perhaps becoming more transparent He blessed me with an awakening. It was time for me to wake up and use every spiritual gift and every resource He had blessed me to reap. I am to use them by listening closely to His voice for His directions and doing what He says, when He says, and the way He says. As I write these words, I have been doing daily devotion (generally about 1-2 hours) for about 934 days consecutively (yes, I followed the advice of my former pastor and recorded notes during my study time). This awesome time of study and devotion, is one of the ways in which the Lord has been (and I believe will continue) speaking to me. In terms of being transparent, I very frankly have not been the man I should have been. In the various areas of my life, I have not taken the stand I should have taken; have not done what I should have done; have not said what I should have said or gone where I should have gone. I have actually lived my life, like Timothy once did, timidly. Interestingly enough one of the scriptures that has been a big part of my devotion time is II Timothy 1:7; For God has not given us a spirit of fear, but of power and love and a sound mind. What a reaping season this is about to become. The hotel where I wrote these words was very nice as was the suite where I sat as I wrote. My wife was resting in the bedroom and truly had no clue how my life and as a result, our lives were changing right then! I truly was thankful to God for speaking to my heart as He had over the previous couple of years and His speaking with me on that particular morning in that hotel suite as I was doing my devotion. Thank God that He does speak with us, but we must prayerfully do what the Word says as we grow in learning to listen for and be obedient to His great voice.

On our tenth consecutive monthly getaway, as I reflected, I recognized just how much in the previous couple of weeks God had blessed. It just so very much was a clear view of God's blessings. Just a few of the things are our son, CJ taking on full-time employment and enjoying the job. He's been making it to church, sitting under solid biblical preaching pretty consistently. We received great news from my mother's doctors regarding her health. She had been diagnosed with multiple myeloma, but after speaking with her cancer doctor Deb and I were very encouraged by his report. Also, I spoke with her family practitioner and he had nothing but good news. I met her nurses and aids who come in daily for eight hours and her aide was wonderful. On the day we came to our tenth consecutive get-away we received great news on two fronts, both coming at almost the exact same time; our oldest child, Lauren, learned that she got the job she was praying for and that they were matching unexpectedly, the salary of the job she was leaving. And finally, in the middle of my devotion I received a call from a very strong Christian business owner that he would be leaving his operation and would need to pass on some of his business and that he would like to pass it on to me. This is my Season of Reaping. I had planned that when Deb and I got back in town from our getaway, I would audition for a part in a fairly major Good Friday production in our area. The audition was a good experience for me, but I did not get the part.

Right after God had a Christian brother hand over a ton of customers to me that he would no longer be servicing, God had a neighbor ask me to come down to her shed in the back yard in a couple of days because she was going to clean it out and believed that there may be a number of things in the shed that I could use in my business. I was blown away by what I found. Numerous items that were a tremendous blessing to Due Season Lawns. What is interesting to me is that because God had been allowing me tremendous study/devotion time, I had just started to see and understand so many things in scripture. In terms of my neighbor opening her shed to me, and to give to me at an incredibly low cost many items for my business, my mind went to what I read numerous times regarding how Moses' sister was told by the Queen to find a nurse for Moses—she found someone alright…Moses' mother!! One commentary that I had read over and over suggested that we must always be careful not to overlook the miraculous way that God may be wanting to bless us…even when we may not expect it to unfold that way. My mom did soon after her diagnosis end up going home to be with the Lord. She passed, but even in her falling asleep in Christ, she was still leading others to Christ, even one lady who was on her death bed and passed shortly after mom lead her to Christ. My mom didn't tell me this… one of her nurses did. Also, even though I didn't get the part I had auditioned for, my wife later talked me into auditioning for a play at our local community theater, and by the grace of God I did get the part and we did eleven performances of the production in April of 2024. By the way our daughter has had a couple of more promotions and is blessed to be buying a brand new single family home.

I very seriously have decided that I just cannot keep up with the number of ways God is blessing Debra and me in this reaping season. One thing for sure though is that we know He truly is doing just that…blessing us mightily in this great Season of Reaping.

Reason for the Season - #1

Consider this...
"Do you want to be greatly blessed?
Then sow like it!"

Prosperity is not just about business, but is truly much more about sowing,
About being used by Me and at the same time about growing.
The great things I have for you, I am releasing even now,
In a way that is becoming quite clear to you...I'm already showing you how.

As you have for so long been giving, there was never a time when I lost track.
Now, expect to be blessed because I know "how to give" and "how to give back".
You may not feel very ready—or that you are worthy of what I have already begun to do.
But relax, it's never been about your ability. It's about Me choosing and then using you.

I'm starting this season in your heart and mind...as great love and peace unto you I give.
Now watch from this moment on, just how much more prosperously you will be able to live.
I know all about your struggles and heartaches, about your pain and your tears,
I even know about your feelings of inadequacy, your concerns and your fears.

I've placed you where you are so that you can without a doubt begin to see,
That what you have begun to reap could only come through sowing and from Me.
I've painted this beautiful picture for you, My crystal-clear sea and azure blue skies,
To speak to Who I am, All-powerful, All-knowing, Omnipresent, loving and All-wise.

I promised Abraham that he would become a great nation as he saw the stars and sands of the sea.
Now I'm telling you that you're already being blessed beyond what you believed you could be.
Observe the deep blue sea all around you…a great sea of which you see no end,
And know that onboard this ship called *Destiny* your reaping season did begin.

To welcome you to this season, great peace you've been given. Expect to receive much more.
Step into your blessed season…by walking through each God-opened door.
No, it's not just about business, but about how you use what I've placed in and around you.
As you truly have sown, have done what I said, have done what I've asked you to.

In life one does reap as he has sown. I welcome you to your reaping season.
Begin to look at how much you are being blessed…and know that your sowing is one reason.

ABUNDANTLY

God longs to bless you. He is not, however, going to automatically bless you just because you are a good businessperson or just because you have become very skilled at any particular thing. He is going to bless you because you are using that which He has blessed you with…because you are using it to be a blessing to others and for His glory. As you have made yourself available and have been used by God, He has allowed you to grow spiritually, positioning you for this time, this special time that He has chosen to usher you into your season of reaping. Understand that the peace and joy that you are experiencing are not just by chance and neither is the beauty of God's creation which He has lovingly framed for your viewing pleasure and for your understanding of this moment. He is allowing you to go where you go and do what you do, in order for you to experience the peace and joy you now know. He is allowing you to see what you see so that you have no doubt that it is God Who is blessing you. It is God Who is blessing you! Over the years, He has seen the way you have had a heart for the kingdom, and have given of your time, talent, and treasure accordingly. He knows that you love Him and knows that you love His people, the very people He created and loves more than you, on this side of heaven, ever could. He has seen and taken note of the things you do which demonstrate your love for Him and for them. You've been planting seeds for a while now and God has noticed each time you did. Because He has seen your faithfulness, God Who is able to bless you abundantly, exceedingly above all you could ask or think, is giving back to you a similar blessing to what you have given and the blessing you have been for the sake of the kingdom. He is going to give you that part back and then is going to give you more. When you gave, you gave from your heart and were not giving as an investment. You weren't giving to get something back. You were not investing. You were giving. You gave from a heart of love. That is the reason God can bless you the way He is blessing you. And because He created you, He knows (even more than you do) what makes you happiest, what brings the greatest joy to your heart. Child of God, those are things God has already begun to bless you with as you cruise His beautiful blue western Caribbean seas and soar above the fluffy white clouds that add to the great décor of His majestic blue sky. Even though you may not feel like you are ready (in terms of being worthy) for all that God is about to do in your life, just believe that you can look forward expectantly to His continued and abundant blessings. They are now yours. He has opened the door that leads to your abundantly reaping the way you have abundantly sown. God knows that you are not likely to be able to understand why or how you would be blessed so, but don't worry—it's not about your ability. It is about God continuing to use you (and to use you even more) to be a blessing in the kingdom and to His people. Don't you sense it right now in your spirit…the great peace He has granted unto you which is way beyond your understanding. It's okay if you don't get it yet. Enjoy the picture He has painted for you as you recline, relaxing on the deck of a ship called *Destiny*, alongside your lovely wife, His very precious gift to you, as she enjoys quiet time reading and you write these very words that God is giving you, both of you observing the tapestry of the beautiful, as far as you can see, unending crystal-clear blue waters and the majestic sky adorned with its gently white clouds and wearing its calming azure blue so very delightfully. Please make no mistake about it. This is it! This is that moment when you begin to see and to understand blessing and abundance finding and taking hold of you. Expect to live a life with abundance enough to live much more comfortably and even more importantly to be so much more of a blessing in the lives of others and for God to be glorified. Don't even think for one minute that God is not fully aware of your suffering, aware of the things that you have been through. He was there when you sowed diligently and faithfully into the kingdom while right in the middle of your heartache, pain, and tears. He knows that you have felt that you were not good enough, or strong enough, or focused or smart enough at times. He knows that you have, at different times, been very deeply concerned about a number of things. He knows that a spirit of fear has done its best to stay close to you and even to overtake you at times. Not anymore—for God did not give you a spirit of fear. He planted in you a Spirit of power, of love, and of a sound mind. That's why He put on this ship called "Destiny" along with your wife and church family… so that you could see and know that what is beginning to happen in your life is happening because God has released great blessings into your life. Did you get that? God has released great blessings into your life. Why has He done so? Because of His goodness and your faithfulness (He is always faithful). It is because you have sown and sown for a while. What you have already seen…the joy and the peace you've been granted, could only come from what has been sown (already) and could only come from God. God (as only He could) has painted this beautiful setting for you. You are just beginning to reap as you have sown, as you see the great beauty—through which you have been given just a glimpse of God's great glory—just a glimpse! Yes, there are incredible things in store for you. Lest you forget, He did promise and deliver to Abraham a great nation with people numbered as the sands of the sea and stars of the sky. This does just happen to be a subset of the same set of seas He still owns and the same sky He hung in place and that you have been so greatly blessed by Him to view (He owned them then, and He owns them now). As He has revealed in a promise to Abraham, He now tells you that you have already begun to be blessed beyond what you would have asked or thought. It's already done! You are now in your season of reaping…even as you are still learning to sow more excellently. It did start for you on that luxury cruise ship God placed there for you and which He decided would be called "Destiny". What's about to happen to and through you is because of what God has placed in you. Yes, you are becoming a sound businessman. But it's not about being skilled at business principles. It is about sowing and about listening for and obeying God's voice…about using the gift He has placed in you. This is your season to reap. As you begin to see, the more, just how much prosperity you are coming to know through the grace of God, you will understand that your sowing has been a part of your loving God's plan for you and for those that will be blessed through God's using you. Yes, my friend, you do reap what you sow. God knew and still knows the plans He has for you. You just watch and enjoy as those plans continue to unfold.

"…whatsoever a man soweth, that shall he also reap."
Galatians 6:7

✻
GOD'S GOT IT - #2

Consider this...
"The Devil is a liar—
This is too, your season to reap!"

Always know that God is in control and that He truly does have a plan,
Though at times things aren't going so great and you just may not understand.
If God has told you that this is your time to reap...then that's precisely what it is.
Things may not unfold according to your desires, but they have to according to His.

God knows just how to set you up so that you might be ever so richly blessed,
He doesn't just want you to have what's good—He wants you to have what's best.
So don't allow what looks like a setback disturb the joy you've come to know.
Understand that God is at work and if He said it...then it has to be so.

This is your season to reap because your all-powerful God declared it to be.
Don't be overly concerned with delays or any problems that you experience or see.
Just know that God is in control and that your blessings are on the way.
When God has said it's your season you can believe every word you've heard Him say.

OH YES, HE IS

This season of your life, your season of reaping, is surely one in which the enemy would love to see you become discouraged and believe anything but that God has released blessings that are on their way to you. We all know how wonderful it would feel to anyone to have everything fall right in place, to have all things go very smoothly. That would be easy for any one of us to accept. However, our season of reaping will unfold exactly when and how God has planned it for us, by His design, not ours. It is mind-boggling just how much wiser God is than His creation, man. He knows best how to position you to be blessed, and that positioning (whether comfortable or not) will continue even during you season of reaping. Therefore, you must not think that any difficult thing that you go through, or have a difficult time letting go of in your season of reaping is anything other than God having something for you to get from the struggle or something better to replace that which you may have to let go of. If it seems that you are facing a troubling situation, God may want to use that situation to catapult you to greater things. Because He knows everything there is to know (including everything about you and including the number of hairs on your head and the number of each one), He knows how to bless you best and to bless you with the best. Even when something that's not necessarily comfortable happens to you...know that God is at work...creating the scenario for you to be most blessed. Remember that the enemy would absolutely love to steal your joy and leave you doubting and discouraged, no longer believing that God has bountiful blessings headed your way, blessings that come along with a great plan and purpose for your life. Don't worry about anything else—if God has said that this is your season to reap, then this is your season to reap. Don't be discouraged when things don't happen in the timeframe or manner that you would like for them to, or when you run into problems along the way to your destiny. In spite of the delays, in spite of the problems, know that the blessings God has released are on the way to you. If God said it...that truly does settle it!

"...Master, we know that thou art true..."
Matthew 22:16

Your Room is Ready - #3

Consider this...
"How will you know you can fly if you never leave the nest?"

Larry, stop counting on others. It's time for you to look directly to Me.
In this, your season to reap, even greater blessings you will continue to see.
Yes, I have blessed you through others. Be thankful for all that into you, each did pour.
But now you are about to be more richly blessed...about to spread **your** wings and soar.

I have gifted you to do some things well...to write, to minister, and to teach.
But I blessed you the most My child...when I gifted you, My Word, to preach.
"Your gift will make room for you." This, in My Word, you have read.
Room for you has been made. Why? Because you have done as I have said.

You've been loyal where I have placed you. As a result, there you have truly grown.
There you have been so very faithful and many seeds have been sown.
Now it's time for you to reap as you minister, as you preach, teach, and write.
Joy has come to you this morning, even though you've wept through more than a night.

Go forth trusting and believing, and in the ways in which I have gifted you, so do.
And be ever so bountifully blessed...with all the great things that I have for you.

YOUR TURN TO POUR

God has had others in place in your life that you might grow. He uses who and what He chooses and has certainly used people to pour into you throughout your life. Over the years you have been able to count on them. But now, having done what He needed to do through them, God wants you to stop leaning and depending on them and to now look directly to and lean on Him. It's now time for you to be used to pour into the lives of others. You have already begun to experience and appreciate some of the things that God has for you in this great reaping season of your life. You know what those things are. Thank God for them. As wonderful as those blessings are, they are just the beginning. God has much for you to reap. Be grateful for and thankful to those who have sown into your life. Be thankful for all that each poured into you. It is in part because of the role they have played in your life that you are now beginning to be used in an even greater way by God—that you are spreading you wings and beginning to soar to new heights. God does have a great plan and purpose for your life that He is ready to unfold. You are beginning to walk into that purpose and fulfill His plan by leaving the very comfortable nest which you had settled so comfortably into. You will minister in a number of ways to God's people, but especially in that way that He has purposed for your life. You won't struggle to find your place…it will come upon you because of the way in which God has gifted you and because your steps truly are being ordered by the Lord…and because you have been obedient to the voice of God.

"A man's gift maketh room for him…"
Proverbs 18:16

✳ IT'S ALREADY DONE - #4

Consider this...
"GOD is omnipotent, omnipresent, and omniscient.
He is perfect and He created you—
So you…just be You!"

During your reaping season exactly what is it that you are to do?
You are to bring in the harvest, which God has already given you.
You are to use the gift you've been blessed with. That's how it is done.
That's how you (and others) reap the harvest and how each victory is won.

Remember, it's already done. The victory, right now, is yours.
You are like the mighty eagle which spreads it wings and then soars.
Go ahead, stretch out on faith. It's time you spread your wings.
It's time you understand that, by the grace of God, yes, even you can do all things.

Trust God and just do it…those things you thought you couldn't before.
Operating in His power, love, and sound mind frees Him up to bless you even more.
As you bring your harvest in…this is what God says that you must do…
"Seek My face, stay in My Word, and You, God's child, just be you".

For His gift to you is the answer for each of your needs to be met.
And for you to reap abundantly and in a way which you have not yet.

It's Harvest Time

It's upon you now—your season of reaping. You know that it is here and you really do not want to allow this season to slip through your fingers. You have come through other seasons in your life to arrive at this truly amazing one. God has been growing you throughout those seasons. He has indeed gifted you and you are now able to operate in excellence. Again, this is one of those things that warrants repeating...*God has been growing you throughout those seasons. He has indeed gifted you and you are now able to operate in excellence.* Now is the time He wants to bless you tremendously as you exercise the gift with which you have been blessed. Your gift will make room for you—and yours has. Now you must use both the space that has been created and your gift to be a blessing to others as God, at the same time, blesses you. The gift is in place. The favor of God is in place. Room has been made and the gift, you have sown. Yes, the seeds have been planted, have broken through the ground, and are flourishing. Look around you. Now it's harvest time. Use your gift. See it bless others and watch God bless you. It's time for the harvest that comes from the planting, comes from the blessing of God, and comes from growing (from your growing). This is a season in which it's already done! It is as simple as spreading your wings and fully using your gift. The eagle's wing span can reach up to eight feet. Your wingspan, child of God, has no limits...with God as the source of your strength. You have started to do, and will continue to do some things you would have never dreamed you could. As you use your gift with a total confidence in God's ability to use you and as you do what you do with the Holy Spirit of power, of love, and of a sound mind, you are perfectly positioned to be tremendously blessed...and to be a tremendous blessing. All you have to do is listen for God's voice and be obedient to it. Be who God created you to be and knows you to be as you use the gift which He has blessed you...to bless others.

"...for I am fearfully and wonderfully made: marvelous are Thy works..."
Psalm 139:14

In Ways You Don't Expect - #5

Consider this...

"God's power at work in you results in
the fulfillment of the great plans He has for you"

Take notice of how I am blessing you in ways that you do not expect.
This is just the beginning…not nearly as good as it will get.
Just trust Me as I prove Myself and as you see what <u>we</u> are able to do,
Yes, it is My power, but I have put My power to work in you.

Much greater things are coming your way. You will reap as you continue to sow.
And be an even greater blessing because you will also continue to grow.
I know your heart is blessed by the things I am sending your way…
But just stop and think to yourself—"What does the Word of God say?"

The Lord says, He knows the plans He has for you and how to breathe life into them.
Before you were born He was excited for you as He made those plans; they came from Him.
Remain faithful to Him and as His plan unfolds, ever so richly you'll be blessed.
Because He will open the windows of heaven and give to you His very best.

As Never Before

In this, your season of reaping, you have seen God move in your life as never before. Through the seasons of your life, you have seen Him operate, seen Him at work in your life. You have seen Him over the years and through the events of your life very patiently and skillfully bring about a great change in you. Having for so very long been concerned about your circumstances, you have also been hoping for, praying for, and looking for them to change. It doesn't necessarily seem that your circumstances have changed tremendously even right now, but you have (changed tremendously) and that is far more important (for you and to God). And now your circumstances, too, are beginning to change. You are in your season of reaping and are being blessed in ways you did not expect to be blessed and indeed in ways you would not have dreamed of. Try to think back to that point when you knew, or at least believed very strongly that God decided to make that particular point in time the start of your season of reaping. It was special. It was clear. It was truly wonderful and more than likely came at a time when you were not expecting its arrival. But when that moment, that time, came it truly blessed you and in it you were able to see the glory of God in a way that you had not quite ever seen it before. This is truly just the beginning of your season of reaping and far from all that God has in store for you and I believe, more importantly, through you, for others.

"You will still be eating last year's harvest when you will have to make room for the new"
Leviticus 26:10 NIV

Keep Sowing - #6

Consider this…

"'Sow,' you're getting closer and closer
to achieving God's purpose for your life!'"

Praise God for this reaping season. In it you're being blessed in many ways.
But, how might you best enjoy this season and make the very most of its days?
By continuing to sow…continuing to do that which God has given you to do,
Enjoy even greater reaping as even more greatly God blesses and uses you.

Because you are already reaping, continued sowing will bless you the more.
And you will be a greater blessing…even beyond how God used you before.
The more you continue to sow, the more blessed you will become.
It's sowing that got you here. Just look where God has brought you from.

Now is not the time to slow down. Instead, it's the time to really press.
With the way that God has blessed you, how could you give Him less?
Keep sowing. Press towards the mark. You do have a divine purpose, one that is real,
Just keep earnestly sowing and that divine purpose you will fulfill!

Blessings On Top of Blessings

During your reaping season God has clearly shown you that He has the desire and the ability to bless you exceedingly and abundantly. Thank and praise God for that. But what should you be doing with your time during this great reaping season? You love being used by God, especially in the way in which He has gifted you. So, doesn't it make sense to keep sowing, to keep using the gift God has graciously blessed you with? Not only will you experience great joy from knowing you are being used by God, but you will reap countless blessings along with the sheer joy of being used greatly by God as well. In addition to that, and perhaps, more significantly, you will be a great blessing to others. Even though you are already being blessed, there is no better time to sow than right as God is blessing you so, as you are reaping (from that which has been sown before). Then, by sowing even <u>as</u> you are reaping, you give God great opportunity to bless you with blessings on top of blessings. You do reap what you sow. In part, because of your sowing, God has blessed you to reap His bountiful blessings. Should you ever forget just how much He has blessed you, just think back. Think about how far you know God has brought you from. No one knows just how far that really is—but you! He has brought you from a mighty long way, hasn't He? Look how much you have to be thankful for. *"When I think of the goodness of Jesus…"*. Considering where God has brought you from, and how very far He has brought you, now is not the time to stop using the gift God has blessed you with. This is not the time to slow down sowing into the kingdom. It is time for you to continue to sow and to be blessed with blessings on top of blessings—blessings that will overflow into the lives of others, because you are just that blessed! And just think about what a great blessing that is in and of itself—the opportunity to give to others the way you have always wanted to. Besides, with the way God has blessed you, you just can't quit on Him now. You have to keep moving towards that great season of truly *Achieving God's Purpose for Your Life*. He does have a great purpose for your life. If you keep sowing, you'll get there. You will achieve God's divine purpose for your life.

"…I press toward the mark for the prize of the high calling…"
Philippians 3:14

THY WILL BE DONE - #7

Consider this...
"The answer you're in need of—
Pray for it, expect it, then act on it!"

There is much work in this world that God has planned and will do.
And He does have a great plan and His great plan includes you.
You, too, have hopes and dreams, things that you aspire to do and to be,
When your will lines up with God's, those things will become your destiny.

Just seek to fulfill God's purpose for your life and always be in prayer,
Take all things to the throne of grace. God will surely meet you there.
Once you've prayed about your purpose, your destiny, that of which you dream,
Watch out for the move of God, no matter how impossible things might seem.

Expect doors to be opened because with God you <u>are</u> going to make it.
Pray, and when the door opens—act! God brought it to you, it's up to you to take it.

CREATED TO DO THE JOB

What a glorious season of reaping. From the moment it was ushered in you have experienced what a great season it is. Because God has told you that this is your season of reaping, you know that He is doing something very special in your life right now! God's kingdom is a great kingdom and God truly is a great God. He is the One, True, Living God. Our all-seeing, all-knowing, all-powerful (and loving) God has much He has planned to (and will) accomplish. God does have the ability to plan and execute like no other. He has a truly magnificent plan that will be accomplished. Here's the great news for you and me. His plan includes us. He plans for you and me to carry out a very special part of His great and awesome plan. If you are worried that you may not be able to do the job (and it is an awesome job), I have good news for you; you were created to fill the position and to do the job. In life some people just fill the position. You were created to do the job and you do happen to fill the position. One thing that is certain is that we will each face struggles, even during our reaping season. When you need an answer to a dilemma you find yourself in, pray for the answer, watch for the answer, and then act on the answer. There is no force stronger than prayer, so pray for the answer. Seek God for the answer to your problem. He wants to bless you. He wants to answer your prayer and is well able to do so. Here is where it helps to have a will that is lined up with God's will. That is the area of having God-answered prayers, of being able to expect an answer to your prayer. For when your will lines up with His, no good thing will He withhold from you. In fact, He is waiting for you to come to Him for the answer that He has for you. He's already there waiting to answer His precious child's prayer. You **are** precious to Him. After you have gone to Him in prayer, then stay alert for His response to your request. We don't know how God is going to move so we have to stay alert to avoid missing His answer to our needs and desires. Remember, He is both amazing and awesome and just may choose to answer your prayer in an amazing and awesome way—perhaps in a way you would have never expected. When He does answer, then you need to move, based on what you hear from Him.

"…ye have not because ye ask not."
James 4:2

Now Possess the Land - #8

Consider this...
"Your destiny is yours for the taking"

You know that this is your season to reap because God said that it is,
You weren't the one to decide that. This very important decision was His.
Knowing this, what is going to stop you from getting what is yours…
When God has promised it to you and has opened each of the necessary doors?

Yes, it is already done. But there is a part which only you can play,
It is so very vital that you understand now what God has given me to say—
To be blessed with what God has placed right in front of you, being passive just will not do,
God has brought it to you, but to take it…well that part God has left to you.

You have got to fight for what you know is yours. It's your land to possess.
All you have to do is take it. God has brought you to it and already done the rest.
This is not the time to be weary. This is your ordained time to reap,
Knowing that promises that our omnipotent God makes, He is very well able to keep.

MORE USEFUL THAN EVER

Here you are in your reaping season. You have begun to enjoy the blessings God has there for you. But the reason that you are so comfortable in knowing that it is your season to reap is simply because God has made it clear to you by telling you that it is. You didn't even understand, at least at first, how it could be. And no, you didn't get it until God allowed you to understand that the season is about the fact that you have sincerely sown over the years much more than it is about any ability that you do or do not have. All you could do is sow in His strength. You could not have made the decision yourself that this would be your season to reap. Only God could do that. And you know that's just what He did. Now, because you know that God said it is your season, you totally believe and understand that you can take what God has for you. During this reaping season you are already able to see some of those things. The heart of your reaping season is just that close. Why? Because God has led you through the series of doors (doors which He opened) which have landed you directly in front of and in reach of your blessings to be experienced and enjoyed. You sense in your spirit that it is already done. You know that it is. But the land is not going to overtake you. To possess the land (reap the harvest) God has for you, you have to take it. Yes, it is yours but **you** have to take it. You cannot possess the land…you cannot reach you destiny without a fight. Did you think the devil was just going to sit back and give up when you potentially pose such a great threat to what he is trying to do, to his program? Why do you think he is fighting you so hard right now? He <u>is</u> fighting very hard against you right now isn't he? That's because he knows what is about to happen—knows that you are about to possess this land of yours that is flowing with milk and honey, that you are about to be made more useful than ever, that you are about to do much more in the kingdom of God that will prove to be more harmful than ever to his plan and his business of keeping God from being glorified. No, Satan is not happy and will fight you *tooth and nail* to keep you from taking that which God has for you, that which He has right in front of you, yours for the taking. God has done all that was necessary to position you for what is taking place in your season of reaping. God has done His part. Now it is time for you to do yours—time for you to possess the exceeding good land which God has given to you. God has used you to sow into His kingdom, which you have earnestly done. He is now blessing you with your season of reaping. This is not the time to be faint-hearted. It now is the time to fight. It is time to fight for what God has already set aside especially for you—blessings with your name all over them. Remember all that God has whispered into your spirit regarding the great things He has in store for you. Welcome to God's favor and those great things. God has promised them to you and because He is God, He is delivering. You just have to do your part and take possession of what He has delivered, of what He has set aside for you.

"…He will bring us into this land, and give it to us;
a land which floweth with milk and honey"
Numbers 14:8

FROM THE INSIDE OUT - #9

Consider this…
"A real change in you is likely to lead to a lasting
change in your circumstances"

Now that you have been in this season for a minute,
What exactly is it that you've been able to find in it?
Some of the things you expected to see, you are still looking for,
But that which you've already been blessed with, means so much more.

God told you that you're reaping, which you may not have then understood,
But now you actually do get it like you never thought that you would.
For in this season there have been some things that you have been able to do,
Things which God Himself has used to shape, mold, and make a better you.

You know that you have grown, and are much more able than before,
That you have done as you should and stepped through another God-opened door.
The things God has allowed you to accomplish are so that you would understand,
That you are already reaping His bountiful blessings and that you are a better man.

You are reaping right now and He has provided proof that you are doing so,
It <u>is</u> because of the things that you're accomplishing…that you and others know!

ALREADY REAPING

You have been in your season of reaping for quite a while. Now that you have been, what is it that God has done in this season in your life that might in any way resemble reaping? Even as the season started, you may not have thought of it as a likely time for a reaping season to begin in your life, especially considering your circumstances then, and perhaps even now. Considering that this is your season of reaping, you may have very well started it by looking for some sort of material blessings or positive change of some sort in your circumstances. When there are things going on in your life that are not necessarily very comfortable it would be easy to look for a change (for the better) in your circumstances as a good thing to accompany a season of reaping. However, God has let you know all along (and you have read from the beginning of this series) that His concern is much more about what's going on in you than it is about what is going on around you. This will be true in your reaping season too. If you would, just stop for a minute and observe what God has done, not around you, but in and through you. What you have been blessed with that grows you is so much more important in your life than those material things, which just may not have become a reality just yet. God has told you that you are already reaping. You may say, "Reverend Camper, if that is the case then what is it that I am reaping?" You have not seen much of a change in your circumstances and perhaps not a whole lot of material goods have come your way. So, you may not understand this "already reaping" thing—until you take a closer look at what has actually been going on in your life lately. Once you have taken a good look and so realize just what God has done, it becomes crystal clear to you that not only are you already reaping, but you are being blessed in the best of all possible ways; there has been a change (and a great one) in you—a change on the inside. A change in you is much more important than a change in your circumstances. You're beginning to understand how this thing (the blessings of God) works in a way that you never have before and in a way that you never really thought you would. For God has had you do (and accomplish) some things that are different (and to you, greater) than anything that you have ever known before, things that are challenging and things that, unless almost forced to, you would not normally do—things you may not have even (truly) believed you could do. But God! But God knew you could and would do them and wanted you to know that you could not only do them, but do them very well, well enough to open your understanding of some of what He created you to do. God opened doors that (because of fear) you were not even sure you wanted to have opened. But they were opened, opened by God. And when they were opened, you walked through those opened doors (in spite of your fear) and you were changed by each one. You grew! You learned (just some of) what you are capable of accomplishing (actually what God is able to accomplish through you). You learned this, not having known that you actually were able to do these things before due to fear (and perhaps, conveniently, timing). You then recognized that you became a more able man or woman by what God had allowed you to experience—the very thing you were so fearful of. You are excited now because you totally understand that God's Word is so very true, as He told you this is your reaping season. Because you are reaping the greatest kind of blessings from God that you could possibly reap—a change from the inside out! You actually know that instead of operating in a spirit of fear, you are beginning to operate in His power, love, and sound mind in your life. Now, doesn't that feel better? You're not *scurred* anymore!

"For God has not given us the spirit of fear;
but of power, and of love, and of a sound mind."
II Timothy 1:7

Now That You Have Changed - #10

Consider this...
"In life, the better you get,
the easier it gets"

Now that you have changed, now that you know you are able to do more,
It's time to revisit some of the words which I have given to you before.
You are now more prepared than ever you have been,
To follow My Sowing in Excellence instructions as you read them again.

What I blessed you to write in Season of Sowing in Excellence you are now able to do,
Because of the changes which I have caused, My child, to come about in you.
Be excited as you revisit what I've given you and as your memory is refreshed,
Because though I've already given it to you, <u>now</u> you will begin to give life your best.

Although already in your season of reaping, in excellence you will yet sow,
Because of the way I have, through the seasons, blessed and enabled you to grow.
Just put into practice the words that in "Season of Sowing in Excellence" you were given,
And see the incredible change in your sowing, your reaping, and in your living.

God Knows How to Position You

There is always a certain amount of overlap (and some repeating) as you go through the seasons of your life. It indeed may seem that when God ushered you into your season of reaping, you had not yet lived life in a way that demonstrated the title of the season—*Sowing in Excellence*. But God did tell you that you would reap because you sowed from your heart, not because of any true excellence on your part. You accepted that, by the grace of God, this was going to be your season of reaping, in spite of your lack of or limited excellence in sowing. You accepted it, but later on God was going to allow you a peek into His plan for you…for you to get the most out of your Season of Sowing in Excellence, your Season of Reaping, and ultimately, Achieving God's Purpose for Your Life. As much as you wanted to live your life in excellence, it seemed much more like a hope and a dream than anything that might become a reality—this idea of being able to live your life in a more excellent way. But even as God ushered you (as seemingly unprepared for it as you were) into your season of reaping, as thankful as you were for it, you were not expecting much from it. But God! But God had a plan that, like each and every one of His plans, is brilliant. You see, He wanted you to get the most available to you from your season of sowing in excellence. God knew (knowing everything as He does) that the more you believed in yourself and His ability to use you, the more you would be able to respond to what He gave you in Season of Sowing in Excellence. Now, in your season of reaping, God made it clear to you that He blessed you to do some things you never really thought you could so that you would understand that you were reaping in the most important way possible—with a change on the inside. He also knew that at the same time that change would make a revisit to *Excellence* of tremendously greater value. At the same time God was removing the spirit of fear from you, He was preparing you to better revisit and live out your season of sowing in excellence. This is your season of reaping and God knows how to position you to get the most from it. How are you to get the most out of it? By putting into practice the things God has already put in front of you in Season of Sowing in Excellence.

"…that the excellency of the power may be of God and not of us."
II Corinthians 4:7

FLOWING WITH MILK AND HONEY - #11

Consider this...
"God told you it's yours, brought you to it—
Now are you going to look at it or take it?"

God has changed you, has positioned you so that you may, your good land, possess.
You have been made ready, having withstood your trials and endured your every test.
God has done His part so that you can now do yours, and take what belongs to you.
It's time to boldly take what's yours, and to do the great work God has gifted you to do.

Think about what He has already done, changing you from the inside out,
Awakening the power, love, and sound mind within, while distancing you from fear and doubt,
So that you would at this very special moment, as you listen for His voice,
Decide with all that is within you, to make obedience to Him your choice.

You are well able to take what is yours, and to do a great work because of how you have grown,
God, Who is able, is truly blessing you. He's Blessing you to reap as you have sown.
Continue to listen and to be obedient to His voice, for this is a good land He has given you.
It flows with milk and honey. Take it and do with it all that He tells you to do.

It's Yours, Take it!

A great change has taken place in you. You know as no one else possibly could, just how much God has brought about a change in you. But also, you need to know that God didn't change you just so you could be different. He changed you so that you could take possession of the great land flowing with milk and honey that He has already made yours. God knows that now you are ready to do just that, to take possession of the great things He has prepared for you. However, you didn't arrive to the place where you are now by accident. You have been pushed, pulled, prodded, prepared, and positioned by all of the things you have been through. Not only have you endured the tests, but God has also allowed you to grow by providing you with opportunities to take on and challenges to meet, challenges which you normally would have done your absolute best to avoid. God has certainly done His part. He has brought you to this good land, which He has prepared for you. He has patiently made your good land and you ready for each other. He has even gone beyond that and already given you the land. Now you have to do your part and take it. It's right there in front of you. Yes, it has already been made yours, but you will have to do your part to possess it. What will you have to do? It's really simple. All you have to do is—take it! However, you must understand that this is not a passive thing. You will have to be assertive, may even have to fight for it. The devil is not very happy about you getting it, but it is yours and it is worth fighting for. If (especially if) you are unsure about how to make certain you get it, ask God to continue to speak to your heart and when He does, be obedient to His voice. As He has done to get you to this point, He will continue to lead, guide, and direct you as you take possession of the good land He has given you. For a good while now, you have believed in God using you. Now, considering the way He has changed you, you know personally that He is an awesome God and can do anything. You are tuned in to Him and are ready to receive His directions and to be obedient to them. You now listen to Him with a new willingness and ability to trust Him. You are bolder because God has allowed some things to happen in your life that have given you a new level of confidence in His ability use (even) you. So whatever battle you may have to go through to take what is yours, you will—you will stand and fight to possess what God has for you. You will fight and you will come out victoriously and will take possession of all that God has for you and will do all that He has for you to do. This is your season of reaping and you are on your way to achieving God's great purpose for your life.

"Every place that the sole of your foot shall tread upon,
that have I given unto you."
Joshua 1:3

Blessed As Never Before - #12

Consider this...
"Little things done well…
is a big thing"

A change in your ways, in how you think and say and do,
Is the thing that will bring about great changes in you.
There is a special feeling that comes with doing your best,
As in the doing itself, even before reaping, already you are blessed.

Even little things you do well will add to the joy which you feel,
Bring you that much closer to your destiny, and make your purpose more real.
God has blessed you for your sowing so sincerely through the years,
For the time that you've given Him, for the sweat and for the tears.

Now He has brought you to the place where you sow in excellence too,
Because of the change your heavenly Father has brought about in you.
You now find yourself doing what you do in a more excellent way,
And are reaping the results because you've learned to listen and obey.

Continue to sow in excellence in all you do and be blessed as never before,
As God continues to bless you and to bless you so much more.

In All That You Do

How very exciting and richly rewarding it is to do your best in all that you do. You have seen what God has allowed of a season of excellence. You have been changed early in your season of reaping. Now God has had you revisit the *Season of Sowing in Excellence* and you are truly sowing *more* excellently. You are speaking more positively and expectantly. You are believing God for more and you are doing things in a better way. God is using those same things to bring about even greater blessings for you. There is a reason that it feels right to do what you do to the best of your ability. The Word does tell us to do what we do as unto God. The little things you do well will render blessings in your life. However, even in the sowing in excellence itself you are already blessed. Each little thing you do in an excellent way will add joy and peace to your life and will advance you in the direction of your destiny—towards achieving God's purpose for your life. God has made it clear to you that you are in your reaping season because He has seen the sincerity of your heart as you have sown over the years. He knows all about the nights you wept and about just how hard you have worked. He allowed you to enter your reaping season, certainly not for the excellence of your sowing, but because you've done what you've done from a heart of love. However, because God has allowed you to be changed at the beginning of your reaping season and to revisit your season of sowing in excellence, your life has changed and you are now obeying God's voice and because of that you have been blessed and will continue to be blessed as long as you continue to listen to and obey Him. God will direct you as long as you stay tuned to Him.

"And whatever you do, do it heartily
as to the Lord and not unto men;"."
Colossians 3:23

Plan To Succeed - #13

Consider this…

"Plan the little things, do the little things…
What a great thing!"

Now you understand that even little things must be very well done,
For you to finish well this Christian course God has given you to run.
Continue to give your absolute best to all that you do,
And consistently follow God's lead as He guides and directs you.

Oh, how good it is to do all that you do as well as you possibly can,
How much better it is when all is done according to a well thought out plan.
To not only be doing little things well, but to be doing them with reason,
Means God is truly blessing you with a great reaping season.

This is part of taking what God has for you, what He has already made yours,
You have gotten here by His grace, by His opening of previously shut doors.
You've sown and are now reaping. God really is making you your best,
Plan and do the little things, then observe how much, already, you've been blessed.

CHOOSE THE SMALL THINGS

You are so very grateful to God for helping you to understand more fully just how important it is to do even little things well. You recognize that in order for you to complete your God-assigned purpose and to fulfill your destiny you must do what you do as unto God. You must give your best in all that you do. Thank God that He does order a good man's or good woman's steps. In this, your reaping season, He is speaking to your heart, leading you as never before and you are following His lead, listening as never before. You are beginning to recognize the positive difference that results when all things are done heartily—done as unto God. You see the differences all around you constantly when little things are done well. You feel the difference in yourself and you are beginning to see the difference manifested in your circumstances and surroundings. God is also blessing you to understand that if you not only are doing small things well, but have carefully chosen the timing of the small things to be done, then you are truly setting yourself up to accomplish much, to succeed. Carefully choosing the small things to be done simply means making a plan. When you are doing the little things, doing them well, doing them with reason and as part of a bigger picture, you are truly on the path to achieving God's purpose for your life. Look closely at how God is speaking to your heart and realize that this is a great reaping season that He has blessed you with. God is revealing wisdom to you and you are applying (or doing your very best to apply) that wisdom. As you apply each bit of wisdom He blesses you with, you are seeing the positive difference it makes. Each of these things that God is revealing to you strengthen you for assertively taking the blessings He has set aside for you (your good land). To be at this point in your reaping season is a true blessing. All glory must go to God for opening the doors that needed to be open for you to arrive at this point. You know that God is still in the process of making you your best and are able to sense in your spirit that He is not even close to being done with you yet. Here's another one of those things that bears repeating—He is not even close to being done with you yet! You sense it, don't you? Thank God that He allowed you to sow over the years and that now He is allowing you to reap, indeed to experience a season of reaping. Continue to plan and execute little things and see the great difference it makes in your life.

"For the Lord giveth wisdom; out of His mouth

-Cometh knowledge and understanding"
Proverbs 2:6

Now Work Your Land - #14

Consider this…
*"Work hard **and** work smart,*
*Using God's Strength **and** His Wisdom"*

You're in your good land now. It's time to work both hard and smart.
Having taken possession of the land, now is a great time for either or both to start.
Use your good land to produce. Sow excellently which you now know how to do,
Then watch for the harvest. See just how very much God blesses and uses you.

You weren't blessed to arrive at this great purpose to relax. Work is the reason you're here.
God has changed you, has made you ready for it, has removed your doubt and fear.
It truly is a great work—the work which He has for you to do,
Right here, in this, your good land, which your God has brought you to.

If you will now simply put the time in, great results you will surely see,
Putting the time in, working hard, will make you as effective as you could possibly be.
But don't just work hard. Work smart using what you've learned as you've studied God's Word,
And by all that has been poured into you…by all that from God that your ears and heart have heard.

Work your good land and you'll be able to take care of your own, and to give to the poor,
Because as you are reaping your harvest…God will bless you with even more.

Prepared and Positioned

God has brought you to your land of milk and honey, to your promised land. He has brought you to the great things He has had in store for you, and in store for you to do. He has brought you to the land and you have taken possession of it. Now that you are here, where your purpose has been waiting, it is not time to relax. It is time to work, to work—on purpose. It is time to do the great work God has for you to do, the reason He brought you to this good land. He would not bring you here until you were ready—and the land was ready for you. Now you both are ready and there is a truly great work that God is going to accomplish through you. He has certainly changed you and you are ready to go to work. He has delivered you from those twin captive spirits of fear and doubt and you are becoming more intimately familiar every day with those great triplets of His *Power, Love,* and *Sound Mind.* There is a great work that you were created to do and that work, waiting and wanting to be done, is here in this good land that God has brought you all the way into. God has told you before that if you put the time in, He will get the results out. That has never been truer than now, now when you have been gifted, prepared, and positioned by God, to be greatly blessed and to be a great blessing. If you will work hard, put the time in, using the energy God has blessed you with, He is going to do something great in your life…perhaps beyond what you would have ever even imagined for yourself. But remember it won't be about you anyway. It will be, is, and has always been about the work God intends to do through you…the work for which He so greatly and fittingly gifted you, and for which He so fearfully and wonderfully made you. It's about all things working together for good (not for your purposes, but) for His purpose. But God doesn't just want you to work hard. He also wants you to work smart. You are able to work hard using the energy He supplies. You can work smartly using His wisdom—wisdom He has poured into you through study and through others whose voices God used to bless you. Always remember to be thankful to God and to those people. Work smart by taking the time to think about what you are doing as you do it. Do work your good land energetically and wisely. Then God, while blessing others through you, will supply you with all you need to take care of yourself and to be a blessing to those that He wants to bless through you.

"He who tills his land will have plenty of bread…"
Proverbs 28:19

Consider this...
"If God said it, just do it!"

Now, with you in possession of your good land, God has spoken to you,
And has made it oh so clear when He did, the thing you are to do.
You are to use your gift to do exactly as, from Him, you have heard,
Hear His voice and be obedient. You are to obey His every Word.

If you will do as God has said, all that He has put in your heart,
Then you will reap ever so bountifully. But you must finish what you start.
As you exercise the gift God gave you, with your shoulder to the wheel,
You'll experience God's guidance and power; His great blessings you'll know and feel.

You took possession of the land God gave you because of the way you've grown,
And are being blessed, too, God's child, because of the way you have sown.
Now all that you need to do in order to realize the more how truly good God is,
Is to listen closely to Him and then to follow the directions which are His.

Focus on that one thing He told you to do and don't stop until it is done,
Then you will be made much better and a great victory will be won.

A Great Time to Listen and Obey

You know very well that it is God Who has blessed you to make it through all that you have been through to get to this reaping season in your life. You have certainly had you share of struggles. But God has in His great omniscience used each of those struggles to position you to be able to possess (fight and take) the promised land that He brought you to. Now that you have been able to take the land He gave you, God is speaking very clearly to your spirit. It seems that in this season, especially since you've been in possession of your good land, God is very clearly giving you instructions that are straightforward, very doable and perhaps more than likely, even very enjoyable (enjoyable because the use of your gift is at the center of who you are and what God told you to do, and there is immeasurable joy to be found in doing something that comes naturally to you). What He has told you to do, using your gift, is going to be a great blessing to you, but it is also going to make a great difference in the lives of others. The instructions God gave you are to be followed just as He gave them to you and until the completion has been accomplished of that which He has assigned. As you begin to do what God assigned keep in mind that you must follow through all the way to the completion of the assignment. You must stay with it. In some ways staying with it will be relatively easy because you will be doing what you love to do—what God created, equipped, and gifted you to do. As a result of being obedient to the voice of God, you can expect that He will bless you immensely (and very possibly in a way that you would not have expected). Remember that it is because of the way God had been molding you that you were able (in His strength) to actually fight for and take your good land. One of the reasons that God is blessing you so is because you have faithfully sown into the kingdom of God over the years. Your love for Jesus has been evident to all who know you because of the way you have lived your life. What you are beginning to see of the awesomeness of God is just the beginning of what He is going to do in and through you as you go on to achieving His purpose for your life. Your obedience to His voice right now means absolutely everything. Trust Him and do what He has given you to do. If you will just do what He has told you to do, you (and many others through you) will see some things from Him that will truly amaze you (and them). The Lord wants very much to use you and to use you very much. Your will now lines up with His. You have been shaped by what God has allowed you to experience. My friend, this is a great time in your life to listen very attentively for and to then be obedient to the voice of God. Oh, how blessed you are that God is speaking to your heart, giving you directions…ordering your steps. There could be no greater position to be in than that of hearing from God and receiving direction from Him for your life! Since God has given you (and very specifically given you) your task, it would be a good idea to focus on that one thing that He has given you to do. If you already know what that "one thing" is you are truly blessed. If ever there was a case of "Just do it!" this would be that case. If you don't know what that one thing is, ask of God what your gift is and then what He wants from you using that gift! Make it a priority to do and to do well (and completely) what you know God has given you to do at this time. Once you do that you will see how much better you are made by it and will experience a great sense of accomplishment from doing what God told you to do.

"Now therefore, my son, obey my voice
according to that which I command thee"
Genesis 27:8

✳

OPERATING ROOM - #16

Consider this…
"As God continues to meet your needs…
you continue to become more able to fulfill
His purpose for your life!"

In this reaping season, now in possession of your good land, and doing as you've been told,
You see a difference in the way things are going, in the awesome way they unfold.
God told you that this is your reaping season before you could even see that it was,
Things that we are not able to understand, our loving and all-knowing God surely does.

He brought you out of your comfort zone to do things you never thought you would,
Changed you on the inside…the way only an all-powerful and loving God could.
Because of the way He changed you, God was able to then give you the promised land.
Knowing that when it came time for you to take it, how very strong you would stand.

You are being obedient to His voice and He is working in all things for you,
His intent is to free you up, to accomplish all that He has for you to do.
Enjoy this special season in your life as you see God move as never before,
You know He's awesome, now you're a true witness and understand it so much more.

God has blessed you tremendously. From some heavy burdens, you have been freed.
And you already know that He who the Son sets free is the one who is free indeed.
God is freeing you up to operate, to exercise the gift with which you've been blessed,
And that's why He's answering your prayers—so you can give to Him your best.

OPERATING AT YOUR BEST

You have taken possession of the promises of God that He had just for you. Having taken your promised land, God is now giving you explicit instructions to operate in the good land He has made yours. Because of your obedience to Him, He is blessing you in a most powerful way. You are beginning to see some things unfold that you had been waiting to see happen in your life for (what at least seems like) a mighty long time. As you look back, you remember how when this season did begin, it did not seem to be such a likely thing that you would be entering a season of reaping. It, in fact, seemed like a very unlikely thing. Your circumstances at that time would not have dictated that your season of reaping would be anywhere near. But mans' way (that's you and me and everybody else) is not God's way—and He knew (in spite of your circumstances) that point in time a while back was indeed the beginning of your season of reaping. God went on to change you on the inside, making you ready to take the promise land in front of you…that He had already made yours…yours for the taking. He had to get you out of your comfort zone for your own growth. And you did grow as a result of the challenges you accepted. Meeting those challenges gave you what God knew you needed to be able to fight for and take the promised land He had for you. God knew that you would only be able to enjoy the good things He had for you if you were willing to fight to take them. He had already made them yours, but you would have to fight to take possession of them…and He knew you would—knew that you would fight to take them! You are being obedient to the instructions God is giving you and He is blessing you in a great way. There are issues you have been dealing with for a very long time that God has already started to clear up in your life. He is clearing them up to free you up to better serve Him, to do the great work He has for you to do—here in your promise land where He is going to be using you on a whole new and considerably higher level. You had already known that God is awesome, but because of the way He is moving in this season, you know as never before. You know that God has freed you up from some things which have been making it difficult, and would continue to make it difficult for you to operate on the level that He has planned for you. There are some relationships that you needed to change or end and there are some issues that you needed to be delivered from. God is doing both, settling those relationships and resolving those issues. It is His intention to give you operating room—room to use the gift He blessed you with. He knows that for you to give Him your best, you needed to be freed from some things. You are about to operate at your very best. Jehovah-Jireh is the provider of the operating room.

"…let us lay aside every weight…which doth do easily beset us…"
Hebrews 12:1

Now That You Are in Your Promise Land - #17

Consider this…

"God wants to change some things in your life,
but He wants most to change you!"

Now that you are in your promise land, you're being blessed as never before,
For although God has been blessing you, He's now blessing you even more.
There are some great things with which, recently you have been blessed.
But as good as these things are, they are not the things that are the best.

Indeed, many more blessings, in this great reaping season, are on their way to you,
Perhaps some things you'll receive or some things God blesses you to do.
But the greatest blessing of all is the one that neither of us is able to touch or see,
It's the one that's most important, God bringing about a change in you, a change in me.

Expect God to continue to do great things. Because of Him, you have been changed.
Because of Him your focus is more intense and your priorities rearranged.
This reaping season is truly great because God has done what He purposed to do,
Has brought you to your promised land and made a great and wonderful change in you.

Now with the change that He has made, so much more earnestly you will be able to sow,
And because earnest sowing leads to reaping, expect even greater blessings to flow.

Sow Like You Mean It

God has been truly blessing you in your season of reaping. Having arrived at your promise land and having taken possession of it, you find that you are now being blessed as never before. Oh, how wonderful it is to experience the promises of God as they become a reality in your life. Even now you are able to look back over what you have been through and thank God for those things, knowing that He has used all that you have been through to get you to this point of having fought for and taken the promised land He had—just for you! He has blessed you with some "things", some wonderful things and things for which you are grateful. But as much as you appreciate those things, you know that they are not the best part of what has happened. The best thing that has happened is that God has done first, just what He said He was going to do first. He changed you on the inside—first. In this great reaping season you are very thankful for the things God has blessed you with, for the way He has worked out some things, some situations, in which you certainly needed His intervention. But it seems that, now that you are in, and have taken possession of your promised land, there has been a major change in you. You may not know exactly what happened (or when and what all happened) in you, but you know that God has made a great change in you. You know that, because of the challenges He has allowed you to face and to overcome, your faith in Him has been greatly increased. You had been living your life with a spirit of fear, so very often affecting you and influencing your decisions. But God did not give you a spirit of fear, but instead, gave a spirit of power, of love, and of a sound mind. You have read this and understood it from the Word of God…but perhaps only intellectually. Now you know it experientially because you are no longer living your life in fear. You are filled with God's precious power, love, and sound mind. That, by itself, is better than any material thing you could ever be blessed to receive. Now that you are in possession of your promise land; now that you are no longer living your life limited by a spirit of fear; now that you've been through what you have been through—go ahead and do all that God has for you to do and receive all that He has for you to be blessed with. Sow like you mean it and like God knew you could and would—in excellence. And then just watch what happens! This is your reaping season and yes, you do reap what you sow.

"…Eye hath not seen, nor ear heard, neither have entered into the heart of man,
the things which God hath prepared for them that love Him."
I Corinthians 2:9

IT'S HARVEST TIME - #18

Consider this...
"When God blesses you to take possession of your promise land...
just gather the blessings He has there for you!"

God told you that, for you, He had some truly great things in store,
But it seems that always you were kept from them by what was always another door.
An important door has now been opened and you find yourself in the good land He brought you to.
Right now is the time He's going to do some powerful things both for and through you.

Be blessed in this reaping season as God uses you to do that for which you were made,
And as you are now being blessed with some specific things for which you have prayed.
You prayed for God to change you. So very much you have desired to grow,
So that you could more effectively live your life and more excellently be able to sow.

Well God has changed you, has made you ready for this blessed reaping season.
His great love for you, your love for Him, and your faithfully sowing are each just one reason.
All you need at this time to do, to be ever so richly and completely blessed,
Is to gather the harvest around you, to reap what you have sown, to gather God's very best.

This good land God has brought you to is the place where your harvest, your blessings wait.
What God is going to, here, give to and do through you, will be nothing short of great.
It's harvest time, time to gather. For your destiny, your great reaping season, now is.
The blessings are all around you. Praise God the decision for you to reap those blessings was His.

You do reap what you sow and God has seen you ever so faithfully do what you do,
Now all you need to do is gather the great blessings that He has
sovereignly and with much love prepared for you!

A Promise Land Kind of Joy

You have known for some time now that God has had some very special blessings for you. Somehow you have never doubted that. However, it has seemed as if each time you are close to experiencing a *promise land kind of joy,* something comes along to prevent you from experiencing the great joy that would accompany living your life the way you would truly love to be able to live it. Well, here in your promise land I have good news for you. Now, with you having followed God's directions and having fought (according to His directions) to take possession of your promise land, there is nothing to prevent you from possessing all that God has for you—not only all the great things He has for you to do, but also all the awesome things He simply has for you. His great plan for your life has been leading up to this…to this time when you are truly ready and able to do the great work for which you were created. Part of the reason you are ready now is because of the change which has taken place in you. You have known and prayed about some things you have been wanting God to change in you for a long time. Well in this great season of reaping God has done just that…He has truly changed you and you are now well able to do that which to you has been assigned. There are reasons (beside your having asked God) that you have changed. There are reasons you are so blessed as to be here in your promise land and in possession of it. Let me share what I believe three of those reasons might be. To begin with, God's great love for you; secondly your love for Him; and finally, because of the way you have sincerely sown into the lives of others over the years. You have wanted so very much to be used by God to make a great difference in the lives of others, spiritually and otherwise. You have really desired to live your life in a more excellent way. Now God has changed you and you are ready to live in a most blessed way in this season of reaping. For you to be truly blessed right now, the only thing you need to do is to harvest (gather) the blessings that God has already made yours and that are all around you and available to you—right now! You will simply be reaping, with God's blessings that which will perfectly suit you and the work He has for you. You will be reaping what you have sown. Your sowing has been seen, recognized by God. God has always had in mind to give you His best and now all you have to do is gather the blessings that He has already made yours. The place to which God has brought you, your promise land, is the place where your blessings, the ones which seem to have eluded you, are waiting for you…waiting for you, the one who God designed them for. What others are going to see God do through you is going to be something very special as you will be doing just what He created and gifted you to do. Here again is one of those things worthy of repeating…What others are going to see God do through you is going to be something very special as you will be doing just what He created and gifted you to do. He is going to use you greatly, the way you have for so long wanted Him to and prayed that He would. Child of God, it's harvest time. Time to gather all that God has for you and for you to do. Begin to truly fulfill your destiny… to the point where you know that it is exactly what is happening because of the sheer joy it brings to you and the way it blesses others so. It doesn't matter what scale it is on…you'll know, perhaps speaking silently, "I was destined by God to do this!" Believe it or not, it really isn't that complicated because simply put, what you will be experiencing will be God's plan for your life. It will be Him Who made the decision that you are to reap, to be blessed the way you are being blessed. Remember that God has been there as you have sown through the years and even through the tears. Yes, you do reap what you sow and weeping may last all night but the morning does introduce joy. And yes, it is true that God looks at the heart while man looks at the outer man. God has indeed seen your heart as, while yet making mistakes, you have sown with a love for people and for the kingdom. He is happy to make the decision for you to reap the great blessings that He has especially for you!

"If the Lord delight in us, then He will bring us into this land,
and give it to us; a land which floweth with milk and honey."
Numbers 14:8

LOVE YOU SO MUCH...
I DO! - #19

Consider this...
"For real, A man that findeth a wife findeth a good thing"

My dearest Debra, my blessing, and very precious wife,
My best friend, my lover and the true joy of my life.
In this season God is truly blessing me my love, but He blessed me before—
When I just asked Him for a good wife and He gave me so much more.

Although I can't explain it and it's still a mystery to me,
I find that wherever I am, is where I long for you to be.
I'm such a happy camper when I'm with you, enjoying your company just that much.
Your beautiful smile, your love, your beauty, your warm and gentle touch.

So yes, God has blessed me by allowing me to become one with you,
Debra, I just love you so much and you will see just how much I do.
For God is still working on me, making me a better man,
So that I can continue to love you better. It's because of Him that I can.

You are a good wife, but in you there is so much more that I see,
I do believe that God custom designed you because He decided that He'd bless me.
This is my reaping season and in it I've been truly blessed,
But back when you said, "I do"—well that's when I received His best.

Through the seasons of my life, I am so thankful to you for being there,
For your love, kindness, and passion, and the selfless and deeply compassionate way you care.
I do love you Mrs. Camper and oh how I thank God for you too,
When I tell you that I love you, please know that with all that is in me, I do!

I'm Just Blessed

When it comes to having Debra as my wife, the only way I can put it is that…"I am just blessed". I know that God has truly favored me. The Word does say that a man who finds a wife, finds a good thing. I am so glad that God allowed me to find this lovely, sweet, deeply compassionate lady, my wife, my good thing, Debra. She absolutely is my very best friend. I still get excited about spending time with her doing all that we do together. Whether it is something we choose to do or something we simply have to take care of, I enjoy so very much my time with her. She is my best friend and she is the woman who does still make my heart skip a beat and my knees weak. She is my friend and she is my lover. She doesn't just add joy to my life—she is the joy of my life. I have been blessed by God beyond what I asked for or expected in a wife. I never thought that I would find so much joy in being the "Mr." in "Mr. and Mrs. Camper" or in church life the "Brother" in "Brother and Sister Camper". I am not yet able to understand or explain the joy I feel when I am with this lovely lady, by "boo" (yes, still my boo), Debra. It is however, a joy that is so great that I want to be with her just about all the time. There are very likely many times when the "prudent" thing to do would be for us to go separate ways to accomplish what we need to do or for just her or just me go to take care of something. That's the way, perhaps, that it should be. But the reality of it is that just about every time that situation arises (where on paper, "solo" would be the way to go) we end up doing whatever it is that "one of us" needs to do—together! If I tried to explain why I enjoy being around her so much, I guess it would have to include things like her heart-warming smile (which blew me away the very first time I met her), knowing how much and how deeply she loves me (what a comforting feeling that is), and the deep compassion that she has for people. I stated in my dedication to her in "…*if* You Faint Not" that she is the most deeply compassionate person I have ever met. She still is! Indeed, God has blessed me by allowing me the privilege of hearing her say "yes" when I found her and asked her to be my wife. I just don't think it's possible right now for her to know how very much I love her. I guess the Word does make it clear that it actually is a mystery, as is the way Christ loves the church. I may not understand either fully, but I am thankful for both…my love for her and Christ's love for the church, His bride and my bride. God is still working on me, making me a better man, which also continues making me better able to be the husband God would have me be to Debra. I truly believe that as God continues to bless me and as my seasons change, I will be able the more to demonstrate my love to my lovely wife in ways that I have so longed to. I thank God for you Debra. You really are more than I ever dreamed of in a wife. Sometimes I think that God just had in mind that He wanted to bless me in a very special way and said to Himself, "How can I bless Larry most? I know, I'll give him Debra." He completed that when you said, "I do" at the altar. Not only did you say I do, but you then proceeded to love me and stick with me through each of the seasons of my life, even when it could not have been very easy to do so. I love you so much for that and thank you too. I also thank you for all your love, your kindness, for the way you think of others and certainly for your compassion. I love you precious lady and am truly thankful to God for you. When I tell you that I love you, I just pray that you somehow know that I truly do—and just how very much I do!

"…and she became his wife; and he loved her…"
Genesis 24:67

THIS WALK WITH YOU - #20

Consider this...
"Be glad that you have been through what you've been through.
What you have been through has prepared you
to achieve God's purpose for your life"

Dear Jesus how I thank You for all that You are to me,
I was weighted down by some very heavy weights until You set me free.
I sought You and You answered, invited me to walk with You,
And now You've truly changed me. It's amazing what You can do.

I know that I am truly blessed because You Lord, love me so,
Because You gave me new life, and then continued by blessing me to grow.
In this wonderful walk with You, You have held on to my hand,
And because You chose to not let go, I'm becoming a much better man.

In this reaping season Lord when You've blessed me from the inside out,
You've Taken from me a spirit of fear and given me much to be joyful about.
As much as I am so very grateful for, and do appreciate our walk,
I thank You for blessing me to hear Your voice—and even giving me space to talk.

It seems that especially during this season, I've heard Your voice as never before,
Even now I hear You telling me that this is just a start, to expect to hear much more.
For the season that is in front of me and what You are about to have me do,
Will take everything that I have experienced, will take all that I've been through.

The weights I have had to bear, to be under, to endure, carry and lift,
Have conditioned me to be ready to achieve Your awesome purpose—using Your great gift.
"I do have a purpose for your life" You say to me, "And now you are ready to achieve it.
Because of the work I've done in and through you, now you, yourself believe it"

Continue to walk with Me, listening and doing all that you hear Me say,
And you'll find that the achieving of My purpose is the season underway".

Gifted to Achieve God's Purpose

I am so thankful to Jesus for the place that He now holds in my life—a place I did not always surrender to Him. I know that I am blessed to love the Lord the way I do now and to have the relationship with Him That I have—and to see it growing. God has done some special things for me during this great reaping season. He really has changed me during this time. For that, I am eternally grateful. A number of things that were weighing me down have been lifted off me, freeing me to better serve the Lord. I do thank God for saving me when I was sin-sick and lost and in desperate need of a Savior, as all are who don't know Him. I am thankful, too, for the growth He has allowed me to experience since that time. I have enjoyed knowing that Jesus has been there with me throughout the journey that this life has been. God has truly changed me. Much of that change has come during this season of reaping. When one experiences a real change from the Lord, it is an amazing thing. Yes, He truly is amazing. Believing that God is going to move in your life and that He has a great plan for you is wonderful. Seeing His plan unfolding is, yes, amazing! To be able to feel, know, and recognize the love of Jesus in your life is a great blessing. Thank God for His grace and mercy. His continuing to love me in spite of me is due to no goodness of my own. It is His choosing to love me even though I do things that demonstrate that I don't deserve His love. But, because He doesn't condemn me, I am still able to grow… to become a better man. During this reaping season I am grateful that Jesus brought about a change in me first—before the change in my circumstances. He helped me to understand that the change that took place on the inside was the change that was most important. As great as anything that could have possibly happened in my life, happened when God took away that spirit of fear that had made itself a major hindrance in my life. In this reaping season God has blessed me tremendously and for that I thank Him. I have a lot to be thankful for. I am thankful that I have heard the voice of God so clearly during this season and thankful to know that He has heard (and is answering) my prayers. I appreciate hearing from the Lord and I truly appreciate Him letting me know that there is yet more that He has to share with me…more to say to me—more for me to share with others. I think it is wonderful that He is letting me know that as good as the seasons have been to me, the best is yet to come, especially in terms of Him using me to achieve His purpose for my life. It makes me feel blessed for God to let me know that everything that I have experienced, all that I have been through, was necessary to prepare me for what He is about to do in and with my life. I understand that God has gifted me. Now I understand it better than I ever have and also understand why He did. He did not gift me just so I could have a gift. He gifted me so that I could use the gift to achieve His purpose for my life. He has prepared and conditioned me for the purpose He has for my life by allowing me to go through some challenging things and times. Because of what He has allowed me to endure, He is letting me know that I am ready to do that which He created me for—His great purpose for my life, to communicate the Gospel. It is such an exciting thing to me that I, too, believe that I am ready to go forth and achieve God's purpose for my life. God let me know that all I need to do is to continue to walk with Him and listen for His voice and do what He says and that if I do those things…my season of achieving His purpose for my life will be well underway!

"And I appoint unto you a kingdom,
as My Father hath appointed unto Me;"
Luke 22:29

Printed in the United States
by Baker & Taylor Publisher Services